IT'S TIME TO LEARN ABOUT CUCKOOS

It's Time to Learn about Cuckoos

Walter the Educator

Silent King Books
A WhichHead Entertainment Imprint

Copyright © 2025 by Walter the Educator

All rights reserved. No part of this book may be reproduced in any manner whatsoever without written per- mission except in the case of brief quotations embodied in critical articles and reviews.

First Printing, 2024

Disclaimer

This book is a literary work; the story is not about specific persons, locations, situations, and/or circumstances unless mentioned in a historical context. Any resemblance to real persons, locations, situations, and/or circumstances is coincidental. This book is for entertainment and informational purposes only. The author and publisher offer this information without warranties expressed or implied. No matter the grounds, neither the author nor the publisher will be accountable for any losses, injuries, or other damages caused by the reader's use of this book. The use of this book acknowledges an understanding and acceptance of this disclaimer.

It's Time to Learn about Cuckoos is a collectible early learning book by Walter the Educator suitable for all ages belonging to Walter the Educator's Collectible Early Learning Book Series. Collect more books at WaltertheEducator.com

USE THE EXTRA SPACE TO TAKE NOTES AND DOCUMENT YOUR MEMORIES

CUCKOOS

Hello, young friend, come take a look,

It's Time to Learn about

Cuckoos

Let's meet the bird called Cuckoo, look!

She sings her name from tree to tree,

"Cuckoo! Cuckoo!" wild and free.

She wears soft feathers, gray and neat,

With spots and stripes from head to feet.

She isn't big, but not too small,

She blends in well among them all.

The cuckoo calls in springtime days,

When flowers bloom and children play.

Her song is clear, a lovely sound

You'll hear her echo all around.

But here's a trick the cuckoo plays,

A secret from her nesting ways:

She lays her egg in someone's nest,

And lets the other bird do the rest!

It's Time to Learn about

Cuckoos

That's called a "brood" bird, sly and smart,

She hides her egg, then flies apart.

The baby hatches, big and strong,

And sings the cuckoo's secret song.

The young one grows so fast and wide,

It sometimes makes the others slide!

It gets the food and takes the space,

With wide, loud mouth and hungry face.

Though sneaky, cuckoos aren't unkind

It's just the way they've been designed.

They follow nature's special plan,

Just like a fox, or fish, or man.

They fly alone, not in a crowd,

Through forest trees or under cloud.

They travel far from land to land,

With strong, swift wings and tail so grand.

In summer they are easy to hear,

But in the fall, they disappear.

They migrate to a warmer sky,

And wave the cooler winds goodbye.

It's Time to Learn about

Cuckoos

So if you hear "Cuckoo!" one day,

Be sure to smile and shout, "Hooray!"

A clever bird is flying through

The lovely, tricky Cuckoo!

ABOUT THE CREATOR

Walter the Educator is one of the pseudonyms for Walter Anderson. Formally educated in Chemistry, Business, and Education, he is an educator, an author, a diverse entrepreneur, and he is the son of a disabled war veteran. "Walter the Educator" shares his time between educating and creating. He holds interests and owns several creative projects that entertain, enlighten, enhance, and educate, hoping to inspire and motivate you. Follow, find new works, and stay up to date with Walter the Educator™ at WaltertheEducator.com

www.ingramcontent.com/pod-product-compliance
Lightning Source LLC
LaVergne TN
LVHW051920060526
838201LV00060B/4102